MYSTERIOUS RUINS

LOST CITIES AND
BURIED TREASURE

Natalie Jane Prior wrote *Mysterious Ruins* because she has always been fascinated by archaeology. Her other interests include gardening, theatre, science fiction, and chocolate.

Other great books in the **True Stories series:**

Bog Bodies
Mummies and Curious Corpses
by Natalie Jane Prior

The Cruelest Place on Earth
Stories from Antarctica
by John Nicholson

Monsters
And Creatures of the Night
by Sue Bursztynski

Potions to Pulsars
Women Doing Science
by Sue Bursztynski

MYSTERIOUS RUINS

LOST CITIES AND BURIED TREASURE

NATALIE JANE PRIOR

A LITTLE
ARK
BOOK

ALLEN & UNWIN

First published in 1994
A Little Ark Book, Allen & Unwin Pty Ltd
Distributed in the U.S.A. by Independent Publishers Group, 814 North Franklin Street,
Chicago, IL. 60610, Phone: 312 337 0747, Fax: 312 337 5985,
Internet: ipgbook@mcs.com
Distributed in Canada by McClelland & Stewart, 481 University Avenue, Suite 900,
Toronto, ON M5G 2E9, Phone: 416 598 1114, Fax: 416 598 4002

10 9 8 7 6 5 4 3 2 1

National Library of Australia
Cataloguing-in-Publication data:

Prior, Natalie Jane, 1963- .
    Mysterious Ruins.

    Bibliography.
    Includes index.
    ISBN 1 86448 247 8.

1. Archaeology - Juvenile literature. I. Title.
(Series: True stories (St. Leonards, N.S.W.)).

930.1

Designed by Site Design/Illustration, Melbourne
Set in Century Old Style and Helvetica Condensed Light
Printed by McPherson's Printing Group, Victoria

Picture Credits:

• Glenn Beanland: 8 • Coo-ee Picture Library: 1, 7 • The Mary Rose Trust: 4, 5, 6
• State Library of Victoria, General Collection: 2, 3 • Stefan Swadzba: 9, 10

Cover image © Glenn Beanland

(numbers refer to photographs in the color section)

CONTENTS

For Brad

Thank you once again to all the people who helped me write this book: to Linda Miller and Kim Prior for the loan of books and information, Peter Nussey and Andrew Thompson for designing the Auto-Cad pyramid, Sue Bursztynski for the Trojan necklace, Carolyn Hammond and the Barton Library for information on the Middleham Jewel, and the staff of University of Queensland Central Library, State Library of Queensland and Logan City Council Libraries. And also to Rosalind Price and Beth Dolan at Allen & Unwin for their continued support in commissioning and publishing these fun books.

INTRODUCTION

●●●●●●●●●●●●●●●●●●●●●●●●●●●●●●●●

This book is about archaeologists, their work, and some of the places and buildings they have discovered and excavated. It is about romantic ruins, lost cities, and great treasures which have lain hidden in the earth for thousands of years. But most of all it is about men and women who care about the past, and the long-dead, ancient peoples they spend their lives researching.

An archaeologist's job can be very difficult. For every treasure found, years of work are put in, often in harsh conditions such as deserts, bogs, or even underwater. Many times only part of the answer to a question will be found—or sometimes nothing at all. Although archaeologists are always very excited when they find gold and other valuables, most of them are not really looking for treasure. Mostly, archaeologists are concerned with finding out about the way ancient peoples lived.

To understand how archaeologists work, imagine someone three thousand years from now digging up a twentieth-century garbage dump. What would they make of our diet from soft drink cans and styrofoam hamburger boxes? What would they learn about our homes from bits of ancient furniture and the rusted-out shell of an old lawn mower? Imagine them finding an old toilet seat and trying to work out what it was for. Was it a harness for a horse? A ceremonial necklace? Or a piece of abstract art for hanging on a wall? And imagine their excitement when they found personal belongings left behind by twentieth-century people: a set of golf clubs, a baby's bottle, perhaps even an old Matchbox car, an example of a twentieth-century child's toy.

All of the places and things talked about in this book were once built by or belonged to living people, just like us. Men, women and children walked the streets of Pompeii and farmed the rice paddies outside Angkor. They wore the jewelry found at Troy, and worshiped their gods at Stonehenge and in the Mesopotamian ziggurats. They loved their families, took care of their homes, and went to work and school just the way we do. By studying their lives and work, archaeologists can make these long-dead people come back to life.

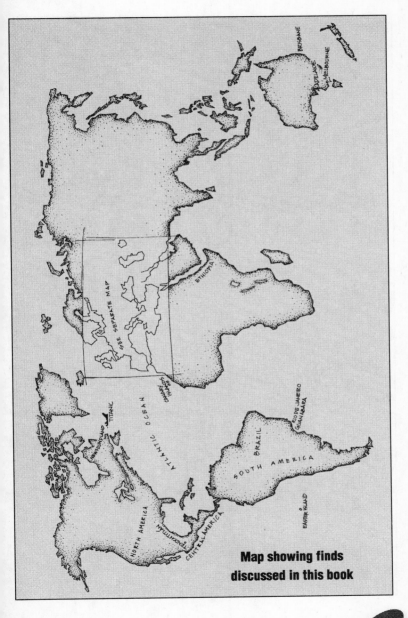

**Map showing finds
discussed in this book**

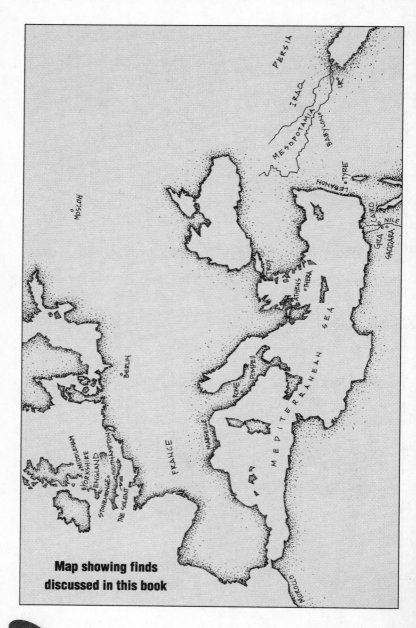

**Map showing finds
discussed in this book**

1

LOST CITIES

· ·

HEINRICH SCHLIEMANN'S CHRISTMAS PRESENT — THE DISCOVERY OF TROY

Christmas is always exciting. But on Christmas Day, 1832, a ten-year-old German boy called Heinrich Schliemann received a present which was to change his life. The present was a book called *Universal History*, and in it, young Heinrich read the exciting story of King Menelaus of Sparta and his long and bitter war against the city of Troy.

For ten years the king and his Greek allies besieged the city, hoping to rescue Menelaus's beautiful wife Helen from her Trojan kidnappers. Finally, they pretended to give up. They sailed away, leaving only the ruins of their camp and a strange wooden horse which the Trojans carried into their city as a prize of war. But the Greeks had played a deadly trick. Hidden inside the horse were Greek soldiers, who emerged during the night, killed the Trojan king Priam and his family, and burned the city to the ground.

By the time Christmas was over, Heinrich Schliemann knew exactly what he wanted to do with his life. When he grew up, he told his father, he was going to find and excavate the lost city of Troy.

The story Heinrich Schliemann read was based on *The Iliad*, a famous work by the ancient Greek poet, Homer. For thousands of years, people who had enjoyed reading Homer's account of the Trojan War thought it was just an entertaining myth. Heinrich Schliemann was one of the few people who was convinced Homer's story was true. He believed that Menelaus, Helen, and the Trojan king Priam were real people, and that Troy was a real place. When he grew up, Heinrich Schliemann became a successful businessman, amassing a huge fortune. But he never forgot his ambition to discover Troy, and when he finally retired from business, he sailed straight to Turkey, ready to dig at Hisarlik — the strange mound which he had identified as the site of Troy.

Heinrich Schliemann was not the first person to think

Hisarlik might be Troy. In fact, although Schliemann took all the credit for the discovery, we now know that he probably got the idea of digging there from an Englishman called Frank Calvert. Calvert had discovered the ruins of a temple and some huge walls at Hisarlik in 1865, but could not afford to dig any further. Schliemann, however, was wealthy enough to employ hundreds of workers over long periods of time, and for twenty years between 1870 and 1890 he went back and forth to Turkey, pouring money and energy into the site in the hope he would finally fulfil his childhood dream.

When Heinrich Schliemann started digging at Troy, there was virtually no such thing as archaeology. For centuries people with an interest in the past had been exploring and digging up ruins, but their work was disorganized, and they often destroyed as much as they discovered. Many so-called 'digs' were simply excuses to look for treasure. But though Schliemann's excavations at Troy *did* uncover priceless hoards of jewelry, he was less interested in gold than in proving Homer right. To do this, he realized he would have to be very careful and methodical. Everything he found — every tiny piece of pottery, every bone, every spearhead — had to be recorded in its place. Because Schliemann had no experience in archaeology, he made many mistakes, and a dishonest streak in his character led him to lie about some of his findings. (Some people even believe his story about wanting to dig at Troy since his childhood was made up.) But while modern archaeologists treat Schliemann's accounts of his excavations with caution, they also give him credit for his excellent fieldwork. Many times, Schliemann had to invent ways of dealing with problems nobody had faced before, and today he is widely known as the 'Father of Archaeology'.

In the 1990s, successive excavations have almost completely leveled the enormous mound at Hisarlik, but when Schliemann started his first serious dig in 1871 the rubble was over fifteen metres deep. Hoping to find Troy somewhere near the bottom, he started work by digging a huge trench right through the middle of the mound. Soon he realized something very strange. The mound did not contain one Troy — it contained several! Over the next twenty years, Schliemann discovered no fewer than nine Troys, each one built on the ruins of the last. Thoroughly confused, but determined to find Homer's city, he finally decided it must have been Troy II, the one second from the bottom. Troy II had been destroyed by fire, as if sacked by an invading army, and when Schliemann uncovered a huge hoard of treasure — gold and silver cups, vases and jewelry — he claimed it must have belonged to King Priam. (Today, archaeologists believe it probably came from the grave of an important, but unknown person.) The discovery of 'Priam's Treasure' made Schliemann world famous, and when he donated it to a German museum he became a national hero.

But did the Trojan War ever take place? To the end of his life, Schliemann claimed his work proved it had, but

> *Over the next twenty years, Schliemann discovered no fewer than nine Troys, each one built on the ruins of the last.*

privately, he had doubts. He could not understand how the tiny Troy II could have inspired the great city described by Homer, and he returned to the site over and over again, hoping to find an answer to the problem. By 1890, Schliemann had switched his attention to the much later Troy VI, but he died before he had a chance to investigate further. Today, most experts believe Schliemann's last theory was right. Greek arrowheads have been found in Troy VI, and damage to the walls once thought to have been caused by an earthquake may have been caused by huge battering rams wielded by Menelaus's army.

THE RUINS IN
THE RAINFOREST—ANGKOR

The trees were thick, and the light on the rainforest floor
was dim. Henri Mouhot kept his eyes and wits about him
as he hacked his way through the jungle, always wary of
the tigers which were known to lurk in its shadows. The
French naturalist had traveled thousands of miles to
explore the rainforest of
Cambodia (then a
French protectorate),
in search of
unusual butterflies
and birds. What
he found,
however, was
something

totally unexpected. As he pushed through the trees to the next clearing, hacking with his machete through the vines and bushes which blocked his path, his eyes suddenly widened in astonishment. Rising above the rainforest canopy were five ghostly grey towers.

Urgently, Henri Mouhot pushed through the rainforest towards the heavily carved towers. The trees grew right up to the crumbling walls of what had once been a vast complex of stone buildings. Overwhelmed, Mouhot wandered through endless deserted colonnades and passages, stepping carefully where the paving had collapsed. Even inside the walls, the stonework was tangled with vines and overgrown with moss, and huge trees had ripped up pavements and knocked down walls with their roots. Monkeys cried shrilly on the deserted parapets, and a flight of bats wheeled, squeaking from one of the towers at the sound of his footsteps. Later, when he returned from his journey, Henri Mouhot wrote that the marvels he had seen that day were unequaled anywhere in the world. He had discovered Angkor, the legendary capital of the Khmer people, which had been lost in the jungles of northern Cambodia for four hundred years.

In the ancient Khmer language the word *angkor* means town or city. Many lost cities are buried slowly by sand or earth while others, like Pompeii, disappear as a result of a natural disaster. But Angkor, for five hundred years the most beautiful city in South-East Asia, was literally buried by the rainforest! Soon after the city was invaded by a Thai army in 1431, the Khmer king decided to move his capital to Phnom Penh, further south. Within a year or so of his departure Angkor was completely deserted, and the rainforest was free to take over.

First to disappear were the houses. Made out of bamboo and timber, they quickly rotted away or were eaten by termites in Cambodia's hot, wet climate. Gradually, the other buildings disintegrated, including the king's own wooden palace. But the temples, courtyards and towers, built in stone to please the eternal gods, remained. From time to time explorers in the jungle stumbled across them, as did a party of Buddhist monks, who used the deserted temples to say their prayers in. They erected huts nearby, and claimed that the ancient buildings had been miraculously put there by the gods. Other visitors were not so reverent. Lured by legends of treasure, robbers came out of the jungle to pillage the ruins. They smashed up walls and floors, set fire to buildings, and broke up statues in their search for gold and precious stones. When they had finished, they disappeared back into the rainforest with their plunder, as silently as they had come.

In the years following Henri Mouhot's discovery of Angkor, interest in the beautiful ruined city grew. Finally, in 1908 a number of French archaeologists began working on the site. They surveyed the city, cleared away the trees, and shored up parts of the ruins which were in danger of collapsing. Soon a picture began to emerge of a mighty city with more than six hundred temples, surrounded by canals and artificial lakes. A moat, filled with human-eating crocodiles, encircled the central city of Angkor Thom, and was crossed by five beautiful bridges. On the outskirts were villages where the ordinary people lived. They farmed rice in water-filled paddy fields, and lived in bamboo houses on stilts, similar to those Cambodian people build today. At its largest, Angkor and the surrounding villages would have had a population of nearly two million — making it a city about the size of Houston, Texas.

Like the Egyptian pharaohs, early Cambodian kings were revered by their subjects as gods. This helps explain the huge number of temples in Angkor. Although most of them are dedicated to Hindu gods such as Shiva or Vishnu, their real purpose was to glorify the kings who built them. All of the statues of the gods found in the various temples of Angkor are portraits of kings, while in the central room of each temple stood a stone 'linga' — a model of the king's penis, which was revered as a holy object. The architecture of the temples was also supposed to be symbolic. For example, the 210-foot high central tower of the Angkor Wat temple represents the Hindu holy mountain, Mount Meru.

Statue of a monkey from a shrine in Angkor

When a king died, the temple he had built during his lifetime became his tomb, so each ruler tried to outdo the last. Apart from Angkor Wat (whose lotus-shaped towers Henri Mouhot first glimpsed through the trees in 1861), the most remarkable temple is probably the Bayon. It has 49 enormous towers, each of which is carved on every side with a portrait of its builder, Jayavarman VII. The expense of building the temples was so great that even though most of the work was done by slaves, the Cambodian kings frequently led their country to the edge of ruin.

During the 1970s and 80s, Cambodia was torn apart by conflict and civil war. The Khmer Rouge, who ruled the country between 1975 and 1979, murdered over a million Cambodians and destroyed many beautiful temples and pagodas. Fortunately, Angkor was spared, and for the first time in twenty years, travelers are beginning to return. The rainforest is full of soldiers instead of tigers, and the unwary visitor has to watch out for Khmer Rouge landmines, but otherwise Angkor is much the same as when Henri Mouhot first saw it — the most beautiful lost city on earth.

CITY OF THE VOLCANO — POMPEII

It was a summer day in August, 79 A.D., and the young slave girl in the plain homespun tunic was hot and uncomfortable. Her mistress, a wealthy Roman lady who lived in a grand villa on the outskirts of Pompeii, had sent her on an urgent message to the other side of the city. The girl was used to running messages and knew all the shortcuts through the narrow streets. Perhaps, if she hurried, she would have time to linger in the forum, look at the shops, and have a cool drink from one of the fountains...

Suddenly, there was an ear-shattering explosion and the girl was nearly thrown to the ground. As she clung to a nearby wall she looked up at Mt Vesuvius, the volcano, looming as it always did over the town.

Above the mountain was a huge, dirty white cloud, and all around her people were shouting and screaming with terror.

The cloud drifted across the sun, turning the city as black as night. By now the slave girl had forgotten her mistress and her errand. Like hundreds of other people trapped outside in the streets, her only thought was to save herself. As she turned and ran, the sky began raining red-hot pebbles. Beside her, a man fell to the ground, knocked unconscious by a falling rock. Then it seemed as if she were fighting her way through a whirling snow-storm. It was the deadly cloud of choking, burning ash she had seen hanging above Mount Vesuvius, now falling on the city. With the volcano's poisonous fumes burning her lungs and eyes, the girl did the only thing she could. She fell to the ground and covered her nose and mouth with her dress. Within minutes her lifeless body was covered with ash. The entire city of Pompeii was buried with her...

Today, it seems incredible that a thriving, busy city like Pompeii could be built at the foot of a volcano. But Pompeii was in the beautiful province of Campania on the Bay of Naples, famous for its blue skies, mild weather and warm, sparkling ocean. People were so anxious to live there that even the volcano's sides were covered with farms and villas! The rich families who owned them probably thought of the volcano as a piece of valuable real estate. Mount Vesuvius had not so much as

> **People were so anxious to live there that even the volcano's sides were covered with farms and villas!**

rumbled for hundreds of years; everybody believed it was extinct.

In 62 A.D. Pompeii was shaken by a violent earthquake and much of the city was destroyed. Today, we know the earthquake was a sign that Mount Vesuvius was waking up. But the people of Pompeii had no way of telling that their earthquake was any different to the others which shook Italy from time to time. They simply cleaned up the mess, and started rebuilding their city. Seventeen years later, when the volcano erupted, some buildings were still being repaired.

Mount Vesuvius erupted about lunchtime on August 24, 79 A.D.. For the people of Pompeii and the neighboring towns, it was a disaster which wrecked their lives. Most of them lost everything they had. A few people later tried to salvage their belongings, but after the earthquake *and* the eruption, most of them just lost heart. The surviving citizens were given homes in nearby Neapolis (the modern city of Naples), and the emperor's promise to rebuild the town was conveniently forgotten. Pompeii was abandoned, and the volcanic ash which covered it was allowed to harden into rock.

For centuries, the buried Pompeii slept. Then, in 1709, treasure-seekers started digging at nearby Herculaneum. These people were not really archaeologists. They were only interested in valuable relics which they could sell to wealthy collectors, like King Charles III of Spain who later financed an excavation at Pompeii. But their work did draw the world's attention to the 'cities of the volcano'. When digging at Herculaneum became difficult (it has a modern town built on top of it), the treasure-seekers naturally turned their efforts to the strange mound which the local people called *la civitá* ('the city').

After nearly 1700 years, Pompeii had been rediscovered. Luckily, not everyone was looking for treasure. As word of the treasure-seekers' discoveries spread, scholars from all over Europe became interested in what Pompeii could teach them about daily life in the Roman Empire. Over the next century teams of archaeologists gradually uncovered the city, and pieced together the details of what the inhabitants were doing on that last, terrifying day.

Because Mount Vesuvius erupted so unexpectedly, people were caught completely unawares. They were going about their everyday business, shopping, visiting friends and relatives, doing housework, even eating lunch! In the scramble to escape, the inhabitants simply left what they were doing and ran, leaving practically all their belongings behind them. This is why archaeologists find the site so exciting. The shops and houses of Pompeii are full of personal possessions such as furniture, mirrors and make-up pots, ornaments, and ancient books in the form of papyrus scrolls. Even food was found. Archaeologists excavating the city discovered 81 loaves of half-baked bread, perfectly preserved inside a baker's oven!

Pompeii was not a terribly big town, but it did have a full range of facilities—a *forum*, or central business district with shops and temples where people made sacrifices to the gods, public bath-houses for both men and women, and a theatre. At the eastern end of the town was an amphitheatre where gladiators fought wild animals like lions and elephants — and sometimes each other—to the death. In the days before newspapers, the walls of the

buildings were used for writing public announcements —
for example, that a bear fight was going to be held at the
local amphitheatre, or that voters should elect Vettius
Firmus or Julius Polybius in the forthcoming election. The
walls are also covered with graffiti. Hundreds of rude jokes
and doodles have been found all over Pompeii, as well as
comments like 'Portumnus loves Amphiandra' and 'Janu-
arius loves Veneria'. One graffiti writer wrote a little poem:

I wonder, wall, that you do not go smash,
Who have to bear the weight of all this trash.

Perhaps the most remarkable discovery at Pompeii,
however, has been its inhabitants. About 90 per cent of
them were lucky enough to escape, and the people who
were killed were mostly those who tried to stay and sit out
the disaster in cellars and houses. (One man died because
he was locked up in jail and forgotten.) In the nineteenth
century, while exploring the site, the archaeologist
Guiseppe Fiorelli discovered a number of mysterious
hollows in the rock covering the city.
Intrigued, he poured plaster into one
of these hollows, and chipped the
rock away. To his amazement, he
discovered an eerie cast of a dead
human body! The ash from the
volcano had hardened into rock
around it, and formed a mould. The
body later rotted away, but the shape

> To his
> amazement,
> he discovered
> an eerie cast
> of a dead
> human body!

remained in the rock, showing clothes, facial features, and
even the hairstyle.

Among the people Fiorelli found were a rich lady who
stayed too long trying to gather up her jewels, and a father

25

who had bundled his little girl inside and tried uselessly to block the fumes with blankets and pillows. In another house two little boys, probably brothers, died with their arms around each other. One of the most poignant discoveries was a dog, left behind by its owners when the volcano erupted. It had been tied up—and was found with its collar and chain still around its neck.

Atlantis

The most famous lost civilization of all time is Atlantis. Perhaps one of the reasons it is so famous is that it is still lost.

Early Greek legends tell of an island civilization situated somewhere in the Atlantic Ocean. Its people were learned, handsome and proud, and they ruled the countries of the Mediterranean Sea as far as Egypt. Then a disaster occurred. Violent earthquakes and a tidal wave struck the island, and Atlantis with its beautiful buildings, fine temples and harbors, sank without trace beneath the waves. The Greeks claimed that the gods had destroyed it for daring to oppose the city of Athens.

Ever since Atlantis disappeared, people have wondered about it, searched for it, and written books about what it might have been like. It has been suggested that Atlantis might have been the Canary Islands, or even America. Another theory is that it may have been the island of Thera in the Mediterranean, which was almost destroyed by a volcanic eruption in 1500 B.C.. One thing is for certain. After so many centuries of imagining, if the real Atlantis was ever found, it would probably be a disappointment ...

2

SUNKEN SHIPS AND UNDERWATER TREASURE

•••••••••••••••••••••••••••••••••••••

RAISING KING HENRY'S
FLAGSHIP — THE 'MARY ROSE'

O n a fine, sunny day in July, 1545, King Henry VIII of England stood on the battlements of Southsea Castle on the south coast of England. Out in the Solent his navy was sailing off to do battle with a mighty French war-fleet. Royal banners of red, blue and gold snapped overhead in the strong sea breeze as the king counted his ships sailing past ... the *Great Harry* ... the *Matthew Gonson* ... the *Great Venetian*. All of them were fine vessels, the best English shipmakers could build. But the most beautiful ship of all was the carrack *Mary Rose*, the flagship the king himself had named after his favorite sister, Princess Mary.

There were many explanations for what happened next. Reports written shortly after that fateful day in 1545 tell us that when the *Mary Rose* sailed out to do battle, she was heavily laden with cannon and crew — up to seven hundred men on board, when the usual number was only 415. The captain of the *Matthew Gonson* later said that the ship was being sailed badly, and that there were arguments between the commander and his crew. None of this would have mattered, however, if someone had not forgotten a basic rule of sea safety. After the ship finished firing its cannon at the French, the gunports were not closed.

From Southsea Castle, King Henry saw the *Mary Rose* turn towards the enemy, heeling to one side as it did so. Normally, this wouldn't have mattered — but the ship was so overloaded with men and cannon that it sat much lower in the water than usual. When it heeled over, the bottom row of gunports dipped under the water, and the sea rushed in. While King Henry and his courtiers (including the wife of the *Mary Rose's* commander) watched in horror, the ship capsized — and sank in an instant.

Despite the loss of one of its flagships, the English navy was able to defeat the French and send them on their way. But the *Mary Rose* was still lying in shallow water off the coast. As soon as victory was certain, King Henry turned his attention to his lost carrack. Sparing no expense, he hired Venetian salvage operators — the best and most experienced of the day — to try to retrieve the ship from the seabed. But the task proved impossible. For many years, the *Mary Rose's* top masts were visible above the waters of the harbor. Eventually, even they rotted away and the ship's final resting place was lost in the cold muddy

Wood from the hull of the *Mary Rose* found by divers

waters of the Solent.

However, the sad story of King Henry's flagship was never entirely forgotten. It became part of local folklore, and in the 1960s an author and historian called Alexander McKee began to wonder where the wreck might be.

In his spare time he read up on the disaster, and dreamed about finding the *Mary Rose* intact. One day, while researching the wreck in a library, he learned to his amazement that the ship had been seen as recently as 1836! Divers John and Charles Deane, two brothers who had invented the first diving suit, had been asked by local fishermen to investigate something which was snaring their nets. The 'something' turned out to be the wreck of the *Mary Rose*.

Bronze guns recovered from the *Mary Rose*

Over the next few years the Deanes brought up several of the ship's great cannon, as well as bottles, cannon balls and pieces of timber from its hull.

Alexander McKee was a keen diver, and with some

friends he explored the seabed in the area described by the Deanes. But the Deanes had removed most of the hull which was protruding from the ocean floor, and in the years since their discovery the rest of it had been covered over. The only answer was to go back to the library — this time to the Royal Navy's chart division in London. Fifteen seconds after unrolling a navy chart dated 1841 — just after the Deanes' discovery — Alexander McKee had his answer. There in the middle of the chart was a huge red 'X' — and beside it, the name *Mary Rose*!

Now that the location of the legendary ship was known, work could begin in earnest. The site was surveyed, and a full excavation began under the direction of Dr. Margaret Rule. It was quickly discovered that the *Mary Rose* had landed on the seabed on her starboard (right) side. In the years after it sank, mud filled most of this side, preserving it from borers and sea water while the rest of the ship rotted away. Using special 'underwater vacuum cleaners' called air-lifts, volunteer divers sucked this mud away, leaving the hull of the ship exposed. Much of the fine work of sifting through the mud in search of artifacts was done by hand, and the divers soon learned to cope with the icy cold water, and having their fingers cut and scratched by broken oyster shells.

In four years 15,000 Tudor relics were brought up from the ocean floor. These included weapons and equipment such as longbows and compasses, and many personal items belonging to the ship's crew. There were combs, gaming boards, musical instruments, cups and plates, and even pocket sundials, which the officers used to tell the time in days before wristwatches! One of the most startling discoveries was a barrel of salted pork with the meat still on the bones after 450 years. The diver who took the rancid sludge away in plastic lunchboxes reported that when he returned from his dive, he smelled so awful that nobody would go near him!

The mud covering the ship had also preserved the bones of about two hundred men. Some bodies were lying on the remains of what seemed to be straw mattresses. They were probably men who had been injured early in the battle, perhaps by French arrow fire, and had been taken below to the ship's surgeon. The surgeon's chest, which was also found, contained some extremely gruesome-looking instruments, including a sixteenth-century metal syringe and a wooden mallet for knocking patients out before operations!

When all the contents of the ship had been taken away the final phase of 'Operation *Mary Rose*' began. Inspired by the *Vasa*, a Swedish ship which had been brought to the surface by archaeologists after 350 years in Stockholm Harbor, Margaret Rule and her team had decided to try and raise King Henry's flagship. A special building with temperature and moisture controls was constructed to house the wreck in the Portsmouth Naval Dockyard, and a metal 'cradle' was made to transport it. When all the preparations had been made, the cradle was lowered to the seabed by a crane and the *Mary Rose* was carefully lifted into it.

The next task was to slowly haul the cradle and ship out of the water. Despite all the care and planning that had been taken, and the millions of pounds which had been lavished on the excavation, nobody really knew what would

Salvaging the *Mary Rose*

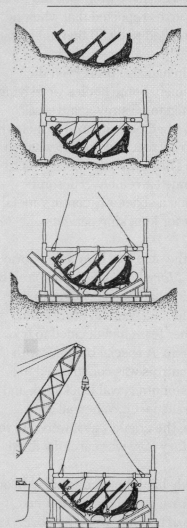

1. First, the sand was dug away from either side of the ship's hull.

2. A steel frame was suspended over the Mary Rose and supported on poles resting on the sea-bed. The wreck was attached to the steel frame with a number of cables, while the sand was dug away from underneath. The cables were attached to eyebolts drilled through the timber of the wreck at carefully selected points.

3. A steel cradle was slipped under the wreck and attached to the poles. Air-bags were inserted between the wreck and the cradle, and inflated.

4. The whole thing was then lifted by crane and placed on a barge.

happen when the *Mary Rose* broke the surface after so long under the water. Suppose it fell to pieces, and sank back to the bottom of the sea? Thousands of Portsmouth citizens turned out to watch, just as they had in 1545 when the ship went to the bottom, while Prince Charles (the President of the *Mary Rose* Trust) stood in for his ancestor Henry VIII. As television cameras rolled, the ship was slowly hoisted to the surface. Apart from a tense moment when the lifting frame buckled and threatened to collapse, everything went to plan. King Henry's magnificent ship, now a skeleton of blackened, sodden wood, emerged from the Solent and was carefully brought ashore.

The mystery of the Roman galleon

In 1976, while spear-fishing off the coast of Brazil, a young diver made a most unusual discovery. On the ocean floor, thousands of miles from the Mediterranean, were dozens of *amphorae*— pottery vessels used in ancient times for storing and carrying liquids such as olive oil and wine.

A pottery expert identified the amphorae as coming from a Roman colony on the coast of what is now Morocco. Unfortunately, it was not possible to properly excavate the wreck, and it is still lying on the bottom of Guanabara Bay, near Rio de Janeiro. But the chances are that in the third century A.D., a Roman galley was blown off course and crossed the Atlantic, over a thousand years before Brazil was officially 'discovered' by the Portuguese. Perhaps, if the ship had not been wrecked, South America might have been part of the Roman Empire —and the course of history would have been changed.

THE DISCOVERY OF THE 'TITANIC'

When most people think of archaeology, they conjure up pictures of ancient buildings, lost cities, and artifacts from thousands of years ago. But archaeology is not necessarily about ruins of buildings, and sometimes it can be used to shed light on quite recent events. When the wreck of the *Titanic* was discovered by Dr. Robert Ballard in 1985, people who had sailed on it were still alive. Today, because of the work of Dr. Ballard and his expedition, new light has been shed on a famous twentieth-century disaster.

The story of the *Titanic's* first and last voyage is one of the most famous in shipping history. When she was launched in 1912 by its owners, the White Star Line, the *Titanic* was one of the most luxurious and expensive passenger liners ever built. Its facilities included huge cabins with period furniture, a gymnasium, squash court and even a Turkish steam bath! As well as being extremely comfortable to travel on, the *Titanic* was one of the safest ships afloat, due to sixteen special 'watertight compartments' in her hull. A shipping magazine of the time even described it as 'practically unsinkable'.

On April 10, 1912, the *Titanic* sailed from Southampton in southern England, headed for New York. On board were 898 crew members and 1308 passengers, among them many wealthy and famous people. By late Sunday night, the ship was off the coast of Canada and heading south. It was a cold night, but people were going about their normal business: dining in the restaurants, resting or reading in their cabins. On the bridge too, all was quiet—though an ominous message had been received earlier in the evening from another ship, warning of ice ahead. In 1912, there was no such thing as radar to warn ships of approaching obstacles, so at half-past eleven when Lookout Frederick Fleet spotted something hazy up ahead he reached for his binoculars. But somebody had mysteriously taken them away, so a few crucial minutes passed before he grabbed the telephone to the bridge.

'Iceberg ahead!'

At once helmsman Robert Hitchens swung the wheel to starboard (right). But a huge ship like the *Titanic* was hard to manoeuvre, and it didn't turn far enough in time. Instead of hitting the iceberg head on, the starboard side scraped along it. Ice flew everywhere, and there was a sound like a piece of material tearing or, as one passenger put it, 'as though someone had drawn a giant finger all along the side of the boat'.

Most people on board didn't even know the ship had been struck. They continued smoking and chatting in the lounges, or slept through the collision in their cabins. But on the bridge, a white-faced Captain Edward Smith already knew his ship was doomed. The iceberg had torn a

> *The iceberg had torn a 300 foot long gash in the Titanic's side, and the sea was flooding into its special watertight compartments.*

300 foot long gash in the *Titanic's* side, and the sea was flooding into its special watertight compartments. While the ship's radio officer started sending distress signals to other ships in the vicinity, all passengers and crew were

ordered to the lifeboats.

Now the awful reality of what had happened began to sink in. To rescue the 2206 passengers and crew there were only sixteen lifeboats, plus four collapsible canvas boats. When they left, more than a thousand people would still be stranded on board. The officers in charge did the best they could, but in the scramble for places some boats were launched half empty. Two of the collapsible boats floated away upside down with no-one in them at all, and when the last boat was launched, it was swamped by the

1500 desperate people still on board.

Seawater rapidly filled the bow of the ship, dragging it under. The remaining passengers and crew huddled in the stern, waiting for the end to come. As the people in the lifeboats watched, horrified, the *Titanic* rose upright in the water. The lights flickered and went out, and there was a great crashing noise as it broke in two. For a moment the stern stood vertical, then with a tremendous roar the ship plunged beneath the waves. One thousand five hundred and three people went with her, and for the rest of their lives survivors remembered the terrible cries of the victims, slowly drowning or freezing to death in the icy Atlantic water.

As soon as news of the *Titanic's* sinking became known, people all over the world started speculating about how she could be salvaged. With all those wealthy people on board, their reasoning went, the ship would be packed with treasure. Weird schemes were suggested for floating it to the surface, including filling it with helium and even ping pong balls! Only one difficulty stood between these people and their dreams. The *Titanic* had sunk in one of the deepest parts of the Atlantic. It was lying in icy water nearly three miles deep, and nobody knew exactly where it was.

Over the years, various expeditions to find the *Titanic* were launched, none of them successful. Finally, in 1985, headlines appeared around the world to say that the *Titanic* had been found. A joint French-American expedition, under the command of Dr. Robert Ballard, had discovered the ship lying on the ocean floor off the coast of Newfoundland in Canada.

Because the *Titanic's* navigator had miscalculated its speed, it was found slightly to the east of its last reported position, which was why previous attempts to find the ship had failed. Dr. Ballard's discovery was also helped by up-to-date sonar and underwater video equipment. A robot-controlled 'swimming eyeball' named *Jason Junior* (*JJ*), and a tiny deep-water submarine called *Alvin* were used to explore the wreck and reconstruct the last chapter of the *Titanic's* sad story.

At first, the expedition surveyed the wreck from the surface. Then they decided it was time to take a closer look. For two and a half hours Dr. Ballard and two other aquanauts slowly descended into Titanic Canyon, where the wreck lay waiting. Minute by minute the water outside their submarine grew colder and darker, until there was no light at all, and they had to put on heavy winter clothing. Attracted by the light, strange deep-water fish swam up to *Alvin*, and glowing sea creatures floated past its portholes. Finally, the submarine reached the bottom. Before them, the black hull of the legendary *Titanic* rose out of the seabed. Dr. Ballard and his companions were the first people to see it in over seventy years.

Before them, the black hull of the legendary Titanic *rose out of the seabed*.

While *Alvin* perched on the *Titanic's* deck, Dr. Ballard's assistant Martin Bowen piloted *JJ* inside the ship and down the grand staircase where the first-class passengers had once walked. He also photographed cabins, and the ship's promenade deck and gymnasium. Dr. Ballard was particularly interested in the gash made by the iceberg in the ship's side, and other damage caused when it sank, because these gave clues to exactly how the disaster had occurred. It now seems clear that (as some survivors of the wreck had said), the *Titanic* had broken in two on or near the surface. The ship's stern had plummeted straight to the bottom of the ocean and smashed into pieces on impact. However her bow section, which was designed to cut through the water, sank more slowly, and eventually plowed deep into the seabed. Scattered all around was an amazing 'debris field' of thousands of objects from the ship.

For hours, Dr. Ballard and his assistants explored in the icy darkness, filming and photographing toilets, bedsteads, bathtubs, wine bottles and china; coal from the ship's boiler rooms and saucepans from her kitchens; even the china head of a child's doll, its body and clothes rotted away. Here and there, pairs of shoes lay on the ocean floor where the bodies of the *Titanic's* victims had rested. But to the aquanauts' relief the bodies themselves had disappeared. Sea creatures had long ago eaten the flesh and the bones had dissolved in the salt water.

Dr. Ballard did not attempt to move any of the relics he found. He felt that to do so was disrespectful to the many people who had died in the disaster. He also reported that the *Titanic* could never be raised. After years on the ocean floor it had rusted to a fragile shell, and the water pressure was so great that any attempts to move it would smash it to pieces.

However, two years after the discovery of the ship, a French expedition visited it and removed hundreds of relics including statues, bottles, an empty safe and even suitcases. Perhaps, some time in the future, an archae-ological expedition will again visit the *Titanic*, and even more of her secrets will be brought back from the deep.

S.O.S.

The *Titanic* was the first ship to use the Morse Code distress signal S.O.S. (Save Our Souls). Until then, ships in distress used the letters C.Q.D. (Come Quick Distress). The signal was changed because S.O.S. was easier for people not familiar with Morse Code to send and identify. (It is written in code as ••• — — — •••)

Alexander the diver

The first person to use a diving bell (a waterproof container in which people can be lowered to the seabed) was Alexander the Great. In 332 B.C., he took time off from conquering the world to descend to the bottom of the Mediterranean Sea near Tyre, now in Lebanon.

3

PYRAMIDS OF
EAST AND WEST

•••••••••••••••••••••••••••••••••

STAIRCASES TO HEAVEN —
MESOPOTAMIAN ZIGGURATS

Once, the story goes, King Nebuchadnezzar of
Babylonia (now Iraq) married a beautiful Persian
princess. Although the marriage had been
arranged, the princess was so beautiful, clever and good-
natured that the king soon fell desperately in love with her.
But though he tried his best to please her, his new queen
always looked sad, and even when he showered her with
jewels and expensive presents, she never smiled at him.
One day, to his horror, King Nebuchadnezzar came across
his young wife weeping alone in a corner of the harem.

'What is the matter?' asked King Nebuchadnezzar. 'Who
has made you so unhappy? Tell me, and he will be
punished.'

'Indeed, O King,' said the young queen, 'nobody has harmed me. But in my homeland of Persia are many beautiful mountains, covered with trees and scented flowers. There are animals and birds, and my brothers and I would ride out on the hills to hunt them. Although Babylon is a fine city, and you are a kind and loving husband, I am homesick for the mountains I have left behind.'

When he heard this, the king sighed and chewed his ringleted beard. The city of Babylon was built in the middle of a huge plain, and there was not so much as a hill in sight for miles around. Yet he could not bear the sight of his wife's tears, so the next day he summoned the royal architect, and told him to build a mountain.

'A mountain, O King?' asked the architect in dismay.

'Yes, a mountain,' snapped the king. 'Like the ones in Persia, with trees and scented flowers. It must have animals and birds and be big enough to walk and ride on. Surely you know how to do that?'

The architect knew that if he didn't come up with a mountain quickly, he was likely to lose his head. So he bowed until his forehead touched the floor and went off to work on some plans.

Soon, when King Nebuchadnezzar looked out of his window, he could see a huge pyramid-shaped mound taking shape on the banks of the Euphrates River: a mountain in the middle of Babylon. On its terraced sides the workers planted gardens full of vines and fruit trees and plants like those which grew in the mountains of Persia. Tame animals were let loose to wander on the slopes. By the time it was finished, King Nebuchadnezzar's mountain had become known throughout the land as 'The Hanging Gardens of Babylon'. And when the king heard the happy laughter of his queen and her attendants as they walked along the terraces, he felt very content.

Today, we have no way of knowing whether the ancient story of Nebuchadnezzar and his lonely Persian bride is true or not. However, the fabled 'Hanging Gardens of Babylon' (one of the Seven Wonders of the Ancient World) really did exist. Ancient writers raved about their beauty, and tourists traveled from all over the world to see them.

Although we don't know exactly what they looked like, some archaeologists believe that the strange terraced mountain built by the king's architect was a *ziggurat*, or Middle Eastern pyramid.

Ziggurats really were artificial mountains, which towered over the flat plains on which they were built. Unlike Egyptian pyramids, which were built as tombs for the pharaohs, they were designed to be used as temples. The first people to build them were the Sumerians. They dedicated their artificial hills to the moon-god, Nanna, and his wife Ningal. Other ancient peoples copied them, and dedicated them to their own gods. By the time the Hanging Gardens came into existence, ziggurats had been built in most of the important cities of Mesopotamia (the land between the Tigris and Euphrates Rivers).

The priests and priestesses, who went up and down several times a day as part of the ritual, must have been very fit!

Ziggurats were impressive, beautiful buildings. Their terraced sides, made out of mud-brick and asphalt, were covered with greenery and other decoration, while at the front, huge staircases with hundreds of steps led up to the shrines and temples on the upper levels. The priests and priestesses, who went up and down several times a day as part of the ritual, must have been very fit! Ordinary people could rest and catch their breath on seats about halfway up. Usually, each ziggurat had about three stages or levels, though there could be as many as seven or eight.

At the very top was the holiest shrine of all: a small room built to be the home or bed-chamber of the god when he came down to earth. It contained a bed with richly embroidered coverings, and a golden table. On special feast days a priestess who was 'married' to the god would spend the night there, in case her husband came down from the skies to sleep with her. The Mesopotamians believed the god descended from heaven to the ziggurat— rather as if he were using it as a staircase. In fact, some ziggurats have names like 'The House of the Staircase of the Bright Heaven', which suggests they really were meant to form 'ladders' to heaven.

One of the most famous stories about a ziggurat is that of the Tower of Babel. In the Bible, the book of Genesis tells how the people of Shinar (Sumer) decided to build a tower that would reach to heaven. But their pride made God angry. He scattered the people, and work on the tower was abandoned. Today, the Sumerian people no longer exist. But the ruins of their ziggurats still stand, towering as they always did above the desert ...

THE POWER OF THE PYRAMIDS—EGYPT

For centuries, people have been fascinated by the pyramids of Egypt. In the ancient world tourists visited them and carved their names on the limestone blocks. Ethiopian kings were so impressed by them that they built them as burial chambers for three thousand years, while in the eighteenth century eccentric English nobles built pyramids on their estates, the way modern people build gazebos. In the twentieth century, some people wear pyramid jewelery, or even sit under pyramid shaped 'energy domes' to meditate. Today, the power of the pyramids over the human imagination is almost as strong as it was in the days of the pharaohs.

That the ancient Egyptians themselves thought very highly of the pyramids is shown by the way they honored their inventor, Imhotep— they turned him into a god!

PYRAMIDS OF EAST AND WEST

Imhotep built the first pyramid (known as the Step Pyramid) as a tomb for his master, the Pharaoh Djoser. His invention became so popular that over eighty pyramids were built for different members of the Egyptian royal family. In later years Imhotep, who was also a priest, magician and writer, became the Egyptian god of medicine.

The largest and most impressive pyramids always belonged to the pharaohs. The most famous of these were built at Giza, near Cairo, by the Pharaohs Cheops, Chephren and Mycerinus. Cheops's pyramid, which is known as the Great Pyramid, is not only the largest pyramid ever built; it is also the world's biggest stone structure. It covers an area of 12 acres, was originally 450 feet high, and is built of 2,600,000 stone blocks, each weighing about two and a half tons! (To get some idea of how big the pyramid is, imagine the blocks it is built of laid out end to end. They would stretch from Denver, to Pittsburgh and back again.) Because the ancient Egyptians had not invented the pulley, these blocks had to be hauled into place by gangs of workers and oxen. Herodotus, an ancient Greek historian who visited the pyramids in the fifth century B.C., claimed that the Great Pyramid was built by a workforce of 100,000.

Many people believe that the people who built the pyramids were slaves. However, archaeologists now think this is unlikely. Some of the workers were tradesmen — stone-masons, artists and sculptors, who were paid well for their skills and lived close to the pyramid in towns built especially for them. As for the laborers who did the hard work of hauling the stone blocks into place, they were probably ordinary Egyptian farmers who were temporarily unemployed. Because the Nile regularly flooded its banks for several months of each year (a time called the 'Inundation'), the pharaoh could call on them to leave their fields and build his pyramid. The men would probably have been grateful for being employed and fed during a time when they would otherwise be out of work. And they would have regarded the chance to work on the pyramid as a privilege; an opportunity to serve their God-King in death as well as life.

After the pharaohs stopped building the pyramids as tombs, they became even more famous as tourist attractions. Greek and Roman visitors carved their names on the stone blocks and named them as one of the Wonders of the World. Later visitors were more interested in exploring the pyramids and finding out all they could about them. One nineteenth-century explorer, Colonel Vyse, even tried to excavate them with gunpowder! When he failed to find any secret chambers full of treasure in the Great Pyramid, he turned his attention to the nearby pyramid of Chephren, blasting away at the base in a vain attempt to find an entrance.

Another explorer was an Englishman by the name of Davison. No nook or cranny of the Great Pyramid was too small or dangerous for him to explore. He clawed his way through bat-droppings 11 inches deep to enter the first 'relieving chamber' above the roof of what was probably the pharaoh's burial chamber. (The relieving chambers were designed to stop the pyramid from collapsing in on the burial chamber.) And he was the first person to properly explore the strange, dark shaft at the furthest end of the Ascending Corridor. With only a candle,

1. One of the many mysterious statues on Easter Island dwarfs a horse and rider.

2. Heinrich Schliemann (below left)spent years digging for the lost city of Troy and was well rewarded when he found a treasure of gold and silver cups, vases and jewelry.

3. Sophie Schliemann (below) wore some of the jewelry found in the ruins of Troy to show its beauty to the world. The headpiece, called The Diadem, and the necklace were made from the finest gold.

4. The raised hull of the *Mary Rose* stands in the ship hall in Portsmouth, England.

5. Many objects were recovered from the *Mary Rose* including this watch bell marked with the date 1510.

6. The surgeon's chest was discovered complete with various medical instruments such as this metal syringe.

7. Cambodian dancers perform at the jungle city of Angkor in the 1920s.

8. The Bayon at Angkor is just one of the buildings decorated with huge, carved faces.

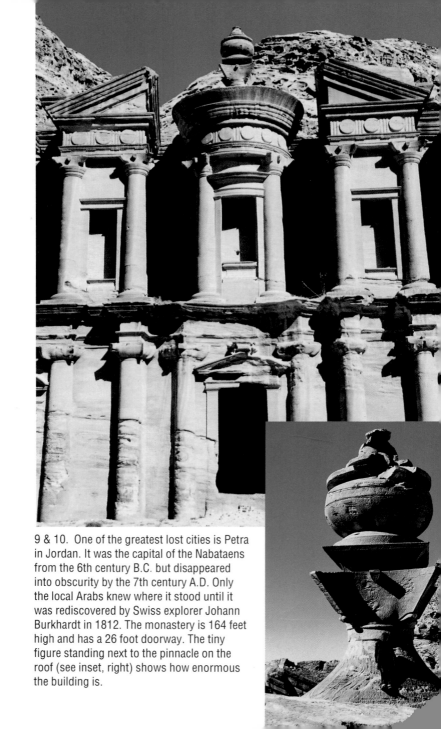

9 & 10. One of the greatest lost cities is Petra in Jordan. It was the capital of the Nabataens from the 6th century B.C. but disappeared into obscurity by the 7th century A.D. Only the local Arabs knew where it stood until it was rediscovered by Swiss explorer Johann Burkhardt in 1812. The monastery is 164 feet high and has a 26 foot doorway. The tiny figure standing next to the pinnacle on the roof (see inset, right) shows how enormous the building is.

Building Cheops's Great Pyramid

1. The Great Pyramid is built on solid rock. To get the base perfectly level, the Egyptians cut a network of channels in the rock and filled them with water. They then used the surface of the water as a huge spirit level, shaving the surface of the rock down to a level plane just above the water level.

2. Most of the stone arrived by boat along the Nile. Workers dragged the stone on wooden sledges up a huge ramp constructed from the river to the pyramid site. As the pyramid went up, the ramp was built higher and higher.

3. From about a third of the way up, however, smaller stone blocks were used. Instead of building the ramp any higher, workers raised the blocks up the face of the pyramid using a rocker device. As the rocker was tilted back and forth with a block on it, timber planks were slipped in underneath, so the block gradually went up.

4. Lifting blocks onto sledges and rockers was accomplished with a 'balanced-beam' — a timber rocker which had the rock hung from one end while the other end was loaded up with lots of smaller rocks.

a compass and a tape measure, the explorer was lowered down the narrow shaft for nearly 164 feet, half-choked by sand and never knowing when his light would go out. Unfortunately the bottom of the shaft was blocked by trash, so Davison never got to find out where it went, but today we know it was an escape route used by the workers who built the pyramid. After the passage to the King's Chamber was sealed with huge blocks of stone, they climbed down the shaft into a lower passageway and made their way out into the open air.

But have the pyramids really yielded their last secrets? And why did the pharaohs stop building their magnificent tombs? There were probably several reasons why the Age of Pyramids came to an end. To begin with, pyramids were enormously expensive to build. By building a pyramid the size of the ones at Giza, a pharaoh could almost empty the royal treasury and bankrupt his country. (This is why the later pyramids were much smaller than the ones at Giza.) The other problem which the pharaohs faced was security. Everyone knew that the pyramids contained fabulous treasures, and some people — the workers — even knew exactly where the treasure was. As soon as Egypt went through a period of unrest, most of the pyramids were broken into and robbed. For this reason, later pharaohs started building their graves in secret hiding places in the Valley of Kings.

However, there is a chance — just a small one — that the tomb robbers may have overlooked some of the pharaoh's treasure. Modern pyramid explorers are just as resourceful as those of the past, and although they no longer use gunpowder like Colonel Vyse to uncover the

pyramids' secrets, new discoveries are regularly reported.
In the mid-1980s two French architects, Gilles Dormion
and Jean-Patrice Goidin, began their own investigation into
the Great Pyramid and how it was built. Together they
traveled to Egypt and carried out 'micro-boring' tests on
the pyramid's walls. Tiny holes were drilled and an
endoscope (similar to those used by doctors to examine
the inside of patients' stomachs) inserted with a tiny
camera attached.

While drilling in the 'Queen's Corridor', the
investigators struck what they described as a 'strange,
crystalline sand'. Could they have found Pharaoh Cheops's
burial chamber? A year later, in 1987, electromagnetic
sensing equipment was used to 'see' behind the walls. The
French, with their Japanese co-workers, had discovered
what seemed to be a room, about 6 feet deep and 13 feet
high—but sadly, it was empty.

The search for new rooms inside the pyramid goes on.
Early in 1994, robotics expert Dr. Rudolph Gantenbrink
sent a tiny robot climbing
into one of the 'vents' which
lead from the room known as
the 'Queen's Chamber'.
Archaeologists have always
thought these tiny tunnels
were unfinished air-vents
(they do not reach the
outside). But Dr.
Gantenbrink's robot
discovered that the other end

But Dr. Gantenbrink's robot discovered that the other end is sealed, not by solid rock, but by a tiny stone door with copper handles.

is sealed, not by solid rock, but by a tiny stone door with

copper handles. Now Dr. Gantenbrink is working on a new robot, so small it will be able to carry a miniature TV camera through the crack around the door. It is just possible that somewhere, behind the granite walls, lies Pharaoh Cheops and some of his treasure...

The English Pharaoh

The Egyptian Pharaohs were not the only people to be buried in pyramid tombs. In 1810, the eccentric landowner and politician Jack Fuller erected a 25 foot pyramid in his local churchyard at Brightling, in Sussex, England. Like the Pharaohs, he was planning ahead. Squire Fuller was not buried in his unusual tomb for another twenty-four years.

Tomb robbers

In Egypt, tomb-robbing was so common that books were written on how to do it! In the Middle Ages, a tomb-robber's 'manual' called *The Book of Buried Pearls* was published in Arabic. It told aspiring tomb-robbers how to find and break into tombs and pyramids, and even gave magic spells to protect them against evil *djinn* (genies) and curses laid by the tomb's owner!

Activity:
Make your own cut-out pyramid

INSTRUCTIONS
*You will need: scissors, a stanley knife (optional),
tape, colored pencils, glitter or other materials for decorating.*

1. Photocopy the pyramid below (you might like to enlarge it) and color or decorate it however you like.

2. Cut out the shape along the dotted lines. Cut very carefully along the dotted lines which form three sides of the door and fold it out along the heavy black line. (A stanley knife will give a cleaner edge, but you can also do it with small, sharp scissors.)

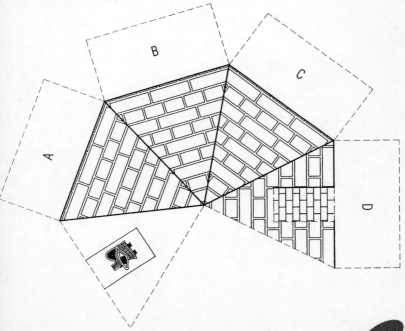

3. Fold the four base flaps. Fold the four sides of the pyramid in along the heavy black lines and position the plain triangle beneath the triangle with the door, so that the rectangle with the picture lines up with the doorway. Secure inside and out with two pieces of tape.

4. Fold up base flap A, then flap B, then flap C. Fold up flap D and tuck its bottom corner under flap A to secure it. (You can make the base sit better by sticking the flaps down with tape.)

Hints: If you make the pyramid big enough, you can cut a slot in the back and use it as a piggy bank. Different-sized pyramids also look good in groups of three, like the group at Giza.

PYRAMIDS OF BLOOD — MEXICAN TEMPLES

The ancient Egyptians are probably the most famous builders of pyramids. But they were not the only people to spend years laboriously hewing and carrying stone to build monuments that have inspired visitors for centuries. Far away, across the Atlantic Ocean in a land that the ancient Egyptians had not even heard of, the Indian peoples of Central America were also building pyramids, thousands of years after the Pharaoh Djoser built the first pyramid at Saqqara.

Carved head from a Mexican pyramid

Like the pyramids of Egypt, the pyramids built by the Maya people of Central America were sometimes used as tombs. But their main purpose was worship — and star-gazing, for the Mayas were great astronomers. Mayan pyramids were tall and skinny compared to those built by the Egyptians. In some ways they are closer to Mesopotamian ziggurats. Like the ziggurats, Mayan pyramids were terraced (usually in three stages), and had a set of steps up the front. At the top was a temple or shrine containing three rooms, with a tall and elaborately decorated roof. The whole pyramid was originally covered with stucco and painted a startling red color — something which the thousands of admiring modern tourists might find rather surprising!

MYSTERIOUS RUINS

In 1949, the Mexican archaeologist Alberto Ruz
Lhuillier began excavations at Palenque, a lost city which
had been rediscovered in the jungle two centuries before.
While exploring in the dim interior of the pyramid known
as the Temple of the Inscriptions, Ruz found six mysterious
holes in one of the floor paving stones. They looked as if
they had once been used to lift the flagstone out of the
floor...When the flagstone was removed, it revealed a
secret stairway, filled with rubble and leading away into the
depths of the pyramid.

For three years, Alberto Ruz and his team painstakingly
excavated the staircase. By the third season, they had dug
so deep that they were actually *under* the pyramid. Then
the staircase suddenly came to an end against a wall made
of rocks and mortar.

Alberto Ruz ordered his workers to break through the
wall. On the other side was a casket containing ritual
offerings: three pottery trays, shells, lumps of jade and a
single pearl. Ahead, the staircase turned into a
passage —and ran into another rock wall. The passage
beyond the second wall was blocked by nearly 13 feet of
rocks. When these were taken away Ruz discovered a
second casket, containing the skeletons of six people —
human sacrifices.

At the end of the passage was a huge slab of rock.
Excitedly, Ruz ordered one of his men to punch a hole in
the rock with a crowbar so he could look through. What he
saw left him speechless. He was looking into a huge room,
its walls covered with beautiful Mayan paintings.

But there was even more to come. In the middle of the
room was a large stone slab covered with carvings. When

Ruz and his workers removed the slab, they discovered more steps — leading down into a secret crypt. In the crypt was a stone sarcophagus, and in the sarcophagus was the skeleton of a man, its face covered with a mask made out of priceless jade. Jade jewelry covered the skeleton from head to foot. Some Mayan pyramids, it seemed, were not just used as observatories and temples. Alberto Ruz had discovered the tomb of a great Mayan ruler.

The great age of Mayan culture ended mysteriously about 900 A.D. Nobody really knows why, although their lands were invaded by Toltec people from the north. One of the more unpleasant customs the Toltecs brought with them was human sacrifice — something for which another pyramid-building people, the Aztecs of Mexico, are particularly infamous.

Aztec sacrifice

Although many cultures have practiced human sacrifice, few peoples have ever sacrificed their fellow human beings quite as enthusiastically as the Aztecs.

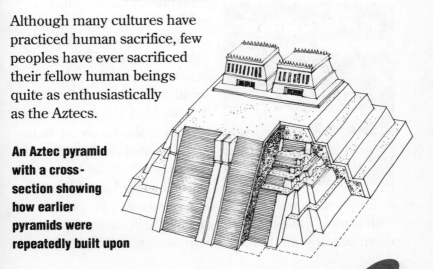

An Aztec pyramid with a cross-section showing how earlier pyramids were repeatedly built upon

To please gods such as Huitzilopochtli the sun god,
thousands of men, women and even babies and small
children were slaughtered horribly on the top of the red-
painted pyramids.

As with Mayan pyramids, the Aztec pyramids consisted
of four steeply sloping sides with a set of steps up the front.
At the top, perhaps 98 feet above the ground, was a temple
where the sacrifices took place. Usually the victims were
captives of war, though sometimes they were children
marked to die by being born on a particular day, or slaves,
carefully chosen for their beauty and grace. The sacrificial
rites used would depend on the occasion. Sometimes,
captured warriors would be allowed to fight a last battle
against hand-picked Aztec fighters, or slaves would be
dressed up as gods and paraded through the streets before
being killed. But generally, the sacrifices were less
elaborate and much more grisly.

> After the sacrifice,
> the dead bodies
> were ... skinned,
> and the fleshy parts
> of the arms and legs
> were returned to the
> victim's captor.

On the day appointed for
the sacrifice, long lines of
prisoners would be led
through the streets of
Tenochtitlán, the Aztec
capital, to shuffle up the steps
at the front of the pyramid. At
the top, each victim was
seized by four long-haired
Aztec priests, dressed in blood-soaked capes decorated
with skulls. While the four assistants held the sacrifice
down over a stone altar, a fifth priest would rip open the

victim's chest with a stone knife, and plunge in a hand to pull out the still-beating heart. With a loud cry the priest would hold the heart up as an offering to the sun, and then burn it in a sacred fire—before moving on to the next victim...

After the sacrifice, the dead bodies were thrown down the steps of the pyramid. They were skinned, and the fleshy parts of the arms and legs were returned to the victim's captor, so his family could eat them with maize porridge as part of a ritual meal. Then the head was cut off, and stacked on a *tzompantli*, or skull rack. When the Spanish explorer Hernando Cortés visited Tenochtitlán in 1519, he ordered one of his men to count the skulls of the recent victims. There were 139,000. Thirty-three years before, when Tenochtitlán's great double pyramid was completed, the celebrations included a bloodbath in which 20,000 people met their deaths.

The Aztec's Spanish conquerors were horrified by the brutality of the human sacrifices they witnessed. Hernando Cortés, who visited Tenochtitlán's beautiful red and blue pyramid, later wrote of 'rooms... full of human blood which had spilled over during the sacrifices'. However, the Spaniards were little better themselves. The invaders crushed the Aztecs and stole their treasure, and their fabulous capital of Tenochtitlán, home to perhaps 300,000 people, was razed to the ground. The Spaniards later used the site for their own city, now Mexico's capital Mexico City. The pyramid itself was almost completely destroyed, though recently archaeologists have discovered the remains of its foundations—ironically enough, beneath Mexico City's Roman Catholic cathedral.

4

MYSTERIOUS STONE MONUMENTS

ISLAND OF STATUES — EASTER ISLAND

Easter Island is one of the most remote and desolate places on earth. Only 13 miles long, it is 2,330 miles from the coast of South America, a tiny speck in the middle of the Pacific Ocean. The land is mountainous, hardly any animals live there, and there are few plants. Geologists believe Easter Island is actually the tip of an active volcano, and that one day the whole island may literally blow up in a volcanic eruption.

Despite this, small numbers of people lived on Easter Island for hundreds of years, eking out a meagre existence by fishing, hunting and farming. They were probably Polynesians, perhaps originally from the Marquesas Islands to the northwest. Few visitors ever came to the island, although in 1774, Captain James Cook called in for food and water on his way to Antarctica. Like other early visitors, the captain and his crew were astonished by what they saw there—hundreds upon hundreds of strange stone statues, standing on stone platforms, staring blindly out over the island.

The Easter Island statues—or *moai*, as they are called by the islanders—have fascinated Western visitors ever since. How could a few hundred primitive people, working only with stone tools, have made so many enormous statues? How could they have moved such heavy objects onto the platforms without horses, oxen, or even the wheel? And strangest of all, why did the islanders, with their limited resources, feel the urge to make the statues in the first place?

Altogether, there are about a thousand statues on Easter Island, ranging in height from life-sized (about 6 feet) to about 33 feet tall. The largest statue, which proved too big for the Easter Islanders to move and is still in the quarry, is almost 66 feet tall, and weighs about 270 tons. Modern visitors tend to find the statues rather eerie-looking. They consist largely of a huge, elongated head with blinded eyes, shoulders and a tiny body, and skinny hands folded across the tummy. The statues look so strange that it has even been suggested that they were carvings of robots made by aliens from outer space! In fact, although the carvings are remarkable achievements, they are not nearly as mysterious as some people like to make out. Similar carvings, usually made of wood, are found in many other Polynesian cultures. The Easter Islanders had few trees to work with, so instead they used soft volcanic rock which was suitable for carving.

Most of the statues were carved by specialist sculptors out of the sides of an extinct volcanic crater called Rano Raraku, and the quarry there is still littered with their stone tools.

Archaeologists believe that the statues were portraits of the Easter Islanders' ancestors—important people whom they wished to remember and revere. Although they look very similar to western eyes (some people have even claimed they are identical), all of the statues are clearly of different people, and when it is remembered that most of them originally had eyes made out of coral (some of which have now been replaced), they appear much less mysterious. The statues were probably carved during the lifetime of the subject, and on their death, were dragged to the platforms by the sea on sledges or rollers. Here they were crowned with a *pukao* or ceremonial head-dress, and erected so that they stared up at the stars.

One more mystery surrounds the fate of the Easter Island *moai*. After going to so much trouble to carve the statues and erect them on their platforms, the Easter Islanders proceeded to knock them down! The destruction of the statues seems to have started shortly before Captain Cook's visit to the island, and probably resulted from the wars fought between different tribes or clans. Whenever a particular clan won, they celebrated their victory by smashing up their enemies' ancestors. By the beginning of the nineteenth century not a single statue was left standing on the island, and it is only in recent years that they have been returned to their places for visitors to marvel at.

THE CIRCLE ON THE PLAIN — STONEHENGE

In winter, travelers driving at dawn across England's Salisbury Plain come unexpectedly upon a strange, even eerie sight. In the middle of a plain of frozen grass, divided only by the road they are traveling on, is an ancient ring of stones. As the travelers near it, they see that some of the stones have fallen, and that they are covered with a light dusting of snow. The rising sun shines dull red through the gaps between the stones. The strange stone circle is Stonehenge — one of the world's most famous Stone Age monuments.

Every year, three-quarters of a million people go to Salisbury Plain to marvel at Stonehenge. No monument is more mysterious. How did the primitive people of early Britain build such a huge stone structure with only flint and copper tools? How did tiny men and women (no bigger than modern school-children) haul giant stones weighing 45 tons each to the site and lift them into place, one on top of the other? What is the meaning of Stonehenge's strange design? Are the spaces between the stones meant to resemble open doors, or a forest of stone trees? Or was it simply a stone copy of similar buildings usually made of wood?

Of all the mysteries surrounding this remarkable monument, the greatest is why it was built in the first place.

Today, after centuries of research, experts are no closer to an answer. They can only guess that Stonehenge was some sort of temple, used in religious ceremonies by ancient British people for over a thousand years. Probably they worshipped sky and sun gods, and held great festivals there on the longest and shortest days of the year—the winter and summer solstices. There would have been singing and dancing, and sacrifices of animals, perhaps even people. But because the ancient people who built Stonehenge have disappeared, and because they kept no written records, it is unlikely we will ever know for sure.

What we do know is that, like many other great buildings, Stonehenge was constantly being added to. First, about 2800 B.C., its builders constructed a circular bank of earth, with a wooden gate or entrance, and a single stone (the Heel Stone) outside the circle. Then, seven hundred years later, two rings of stones were set up inside the bank of earth. These stones (called *bluestones* because they look bluish when wet) came from the Prescelly Hills in Wales, an amazing 200 miles away. They must have made most of their long journey by boat, but the last part would have been over land. Because early British people had not invented the wheel, teams of men had to haul the enormous rocks on rollers and sleds, using harnesses made of leather.

The last sections of Stonehenge to be built were the two spectacular rings of stones which form the main part of the monument. These stones, known as *sarsens,* weigh up to 45 tons each, and it would have taken a thousand workers to move them! Some of them were carved with pictures of axes and daggers. All of the stones seem to have been quite precisely positioned, and probably point to particular parts of the sky at different times of year. For example, the Heel Stone is positioned so that on the Summer Solstice (June 22), the sun rises directly above it. It is even possible that Stonehenge's builders used it as a giant 'clock' to keep track of time by the cycles of the moon.

An aerial view of Stonehenge in one of its many forms

Another stone which was erected at this time is known as the Slaughter Stone, because it looks like an altar for human sacrifice. In fact, the Slaughter Stone was originally one of a pair which formed a ceremonial entrance to the circle. It only looks like an altar because it has fallen over and to the best of our knowledge, no one was ever slaughtered on it.

By 43 A.D., when Britain was conquered by the Roman Emperor Claudius, Stonehenge had probably already fallen into disuse. Although we don't know exactly when this happened, we do know that it fell into disrepair quite early. Stones fell from their places, and were taken away by local people to build houses with, while other visitors chipped bits off to take away as souvenirs. At one stage somebody, we don't know who, tried to demolish it altogether — perhaps because they thought the monument was haunted by evil spirits.

As the years passed, people no longer knew who had built Stonehenge, or why. Geoffrey of Monmouth, a medieval chronicler, was convinced that the stones had originally come from Africa. Giants, he said, had carried them off to Ireland, where they remained until Merlin the Magician brought them to Britain at King Arthur's request. Later, local people called the structure the 'Giant's Dance'. They said the fairies had built it, and that sick people could be cured by grinding the stones up and making them into medicine! More educated men and women thought it might have been the work of the Romans or the Vikings. Strangest of all, one sixteenth-century scholar suggested that the stones were not real stones at all, but had been baked in a kiln!

Some of the first people to pay serious attention to the ruins were the antiquaries John Aubrey and William Stukeley. (Antiquaries were people who were interested in old things, like parchments, manuscripts and ancient buildings. Today, such work is done by historians and archaeologists.) John Aubrey made a famous survey of Stonehenge in 1666, at the request of King Charles II. He discovered a circular ring of pits (now called Aubrey Holes), some of which contained the cremated bones of human beings. (Modern archaeologists think the bones may be those of human sacrifices, or of religious people who wanted to be buried close to the great monument.) Aubrey was also the first person to suggest that

Stonehenge might have been the work of the Druids, the mysterious priest-magicians of ancient Britain.

In 1719 William Stukeley, a Lincolnshire doctor, spent the first of several trips mapping and excavating the monument. Stukeley made many important discoveries, including the Avenue, an ancient road which runs from Stonehenge to the River Avon 1.5 miles away. His work was thorough and exact, and has proved very useful to modern archaeologists, particularly as it records parts of Stonehenge which have since disappeared. However, in later life Stukeley became rather eccentric. In 1740 he published a strange book about Stonehenge called *The History of the Religion and Temples of the DRUIDS*. It was so influential that to this day, most people believe the Druids built Stonehenge. In fact, we now know that the Druids first appeared long after Stonehenge was built. They worshipped in groves of sacred trees, and there is no reason to believe they ever went anywhere near Stonehenge.

In 1915, Stonehenge was bought at auction by a man named Chubb for £6600, as a birthday present for his wife. Three years later, Mrs. Chubb donated Stonehenge to the British nation. Research continues into its purpose, inspiring some very strange theories. People have suggested that Stonehenge is a

> *People have suggested that Stonehenge is a landing place for UFOs, or a giant battery for 'earth energy', which is channeled away by mysterious invisible 'ley-lines'.*

landing place for UFOs, or a giant battery for 'earth energy', which is channeled away by mysterious invisible 'ley-lines'. One of the most peculiar theories was put forward by Gerald Hawkins, a British astronomer. In his book *Stonehenge Decoded*, Hawkins suggested that Stonehenge was actually a stone age computer, used to calculate the positions of the stars and planets.

The numberless stones

According to legend, it is impossible to count the number of stones in Stonehenge, and anyone who tries will arrive at a different number each time. But beware if you *do* succeed in arriving at the correct number. The same legend says that any person who counts the stones correctly will die...

5

TREASURE AND TREASURE-SEEKERS

....

TROJAN GOLD

O ne of the problems with treasure is that everybody wants it. The discovery of a huge hoard of ancient gold almost always brings trouble to those who find it. Who does the treasure belong to? The descendants of the original owner? The owner of the land where it was found? Or the person clever or lucky enough to find it?

When Heinrich Schliemann excavated a huge hoard of gold in the mound of Hisarlik at Troy in 1873, he did not know that his discovery would become the subject of an international squabble over a hundred years later. In fact, Schliemann was only concerned that the treasure should be preserved. According to his excavation permit, half of any treasure he discovered on Turkish soil belonged to him. But the other half belonged to the owners of the land, and to the Turkish government.

Schliemann was afraid that if 'King Priam's Treasure' fell into the hands of the Turks, it might never be seen again. To save the treasure for posterity, he was prepared to do anything—even steal it. To keep the treasure hidden from his Turkish workers on the dig, Schliemann excavated it in secret, and at night—fearing, he said, for his life. Then he smuggled the treasure out of the country. To the fury of the Turkish government he sent it first to Greece, and then to his homeland of Germany.

Some people think that Schliemann meant to keep the treasure he had stolen for himself, and for a while, he did. He dressed his wife and fellow archaeologist Sophie in 'Helen's Jewels', and took photographs of her which he circulated to magazines and newspapers. But eventually, friends persuaded him to donate the gold to a museum in Berlin. Here it stayed in pride of place, in a special gallery bearing Schliemann's name, until the outbreak of the Second World War.

Now the adventures of King Priam's Treasure began in earnest. Because Berlin was the capital of Germany it was heavily bombed by the Allies. For safety's sake, the German authorities gathered thousands of paintings, statues, rare books and other artworks—including Schliemann's Trojan gold—and hid them away. King Priam's Treasure was carefully packed in three enormous crates and stored in an anti-aircraft tower near the Berlin Zoo.

The anti-aircraft tower where the gold was hidden had concrete walls about 8 feet thick, and was probably the safest building in Berlin. No bombs penetrated its defences, and the Trojan gold remained untouched. But by 1945, when it was obvious that Germany was going to lose the war, the authorities in charge of the stored artwork began to worry about something else. The Soviet Army was about to invade Berlin. Surely they had not kept Germany's magnificent art treasures safe — only to hand them over to the Russians?

The German leader, Adolf Hitler, issued an order that all important artworks were to be taken out of Berlin and hidden — in caves, mines, and other secret places. But before the job of moving so many treasures was completed, the Soviet Army invaded. For days battle raged throughout the city and all was confusion. Hitler and many of his followers committed suicide, and two-thirds of Berlin was destroyed. With so many lives at risk, the safety of paintings, statues, and Trojan relics hardly seemed important. By the time the fighting stopped and museum authorities were able to check their storehouse, the Trojan gold had vanished.

> *By the time the fighting stopped and museum authorities were able to check their storehouse, the Trojan gold had vanished.*

What had happened to King Priam's Treasure? Had it been found and melted down by German guards or Russian soldiers? Lost by the Germans during their attempts to hide it? Or had it gone west — sold into the private collection of a wealthy American investor? All these scenarios were possible, but the mostly likely solution was that, like thousands of other German artworks, the gold had disappeared into the Soviet Union. The Russians claimed that in stealing so many German treasures, they were taking revenge for Germany's cruelty during the war.

German 'art detectives' discovered that one of the storehouses the Russians had emptied was the Flakturm Zoo — the tower where Schliemann's treasure had been stored. But no one really seemed to know whether the treasure had still been in the storehouse when the Soviet army arrived. Soon other artworks from the same hiding place began appearing in Soviet museums. But the Trojan gold was not among them, and the Russians denied having ever seen it.

It seemed that the Trojan gold was lost for good — probably stolen and melted down. German experts continued to try and trace it, but in the years following the Second World War, relations between the Soviet Union and the west deteriorated, and dealing with the Russians became impossible. Not until 1991 did the Russians finally admit where the treasure was. It had been stolen from Berlin in 1945 and shipped to the Pushkin Museum in Moscow, where it had remained hidden for over forty-five years.

The mystery of King Priam's Trojan gold is not yet completely solved. Although the Pushkin Museum has not yet put the treasure on display, its inventory does not match the one held by the German museum it was stolen from. Some of the best pieces are missing, and it seems likely that they were stolen — perhaps by German guards — before the Russian army arrived. Even worse, who does Schliemann's Trojan gold belong to? The

TREASURE AND TREASURE-SEEKERS

Russians, who stole it from the Germans? Or the Germans, who stole it from the Turks? All three countries are currently laying claim to one of the world's most important archaeological finds. Perhaps, if Heinrich Schliemann had acted honestly in the first place, the whole mix-up would never have occurred.

Activity:
Make your own Trojan pendant

This necklace is based on a pair of earrings found by Heinrich Schliemann at Troy. (The earrings themselves are too big and heavy for modern people to wear comfortably.)
Most of the things you will need can be found around the house, but you will also have to buy a few beads and sequins. These can be bought from your local art supply shop. To make the pendant you will need:

- an aluminium pan
- strong craft glue
- 3 medium round silver sequins
- 20 silver leaf-shaped sequins
- a small bag of silver seed beads (the tiniest kind of bead you can buy)
- string, yarn or silk cord to hang the pendant from
- a roll of electrical wire
- scissors and a strong needle

METHOD

1. Cut two squares about 1 inch x 1 inch from the edge of the pie plate and flatten them out.

2. Glue the two squares together. Leave to dry.

3. Count out about 15 of the leaf-shaped sequins. They should have small holes at the 'stem' end. Using your needle, carefully punch another tiny hole at the tip. Count out another 5 sequins and put them aside.

4. Cut some of the electrical wire into 0.5 inch pieces. Now join four of the leaf sequins together by looping the electrical wire through the holes at the top and bottom of the leaves. (See the picture for details. The bottom leaf should be one of the five with only one hole.) When you have attached all the leaves together, twist the electrical wire at the back and clip off the ends.

5. Repeat this step four more times so that you have five leaf 'strings' in all.

6. Cut out five small mushroom shapes from the edge of your pie plate.

7. Glue or wire the 'mushrooms' to the tips of the five bottom leaves of each string (the ones without the holes). Decorate the mushrooms by gluing on some of your silver seed beads.

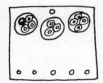

8. Glue the three round sequins on to the top edge of the big pie plate square you made in steps 1 and 2. Decorate them with seed beads and leave to dry.

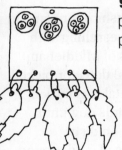

9. Punch five holes along the bottom edge of the pie plate square. Attach the five leaf strings to the pie plate with loops of electrical wire.

10. Punch another hole in the middle of the top edge of the square, and put in a big loop of electrical wire.

11. Cut a piece of yarn long enough to hang around your neck. Thread it through the wire loop and tie off. Your Trojan pendant is now ready to wear.

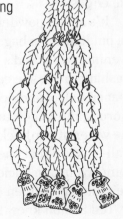

METAL MADNESS

In America, metal detectors are mostly used by
prospectors looking for gold and other precious metals.
However, they can also be useful in archaeology. Amateurs
working with metal detectors around old buildings and
settlements often find fascinating metal relics of times past.
Metal-detecting enthusiasts have helped locate the lost
sites of ancient battles by detecting old cannon balls and
weapons buried in the earth. And sometimes, they have
even discovered treasure...

One such discovery took place in Yorkshire, England in
September 1985, when Ted Seaton went searching with
some friends along a track near the ruins of Middleham
Castle. At the side of the path, Ted's metal detector picked
up a faint reading which told him that metal was buried
somewhere in the ground. The three friends dug until
they discovered the source of the signal — a dirty,
diamond-shaped piece of metal with glints of gold around
the edges.

'It's an old powder compact,' said one of Ted's friends as
he put it into his bag. 'That's no use.' But later that
evening, when Ted's wife was going through his finds and
washing them, she came across the mysterious diamond-
shaped object and decided it was worth cleaning
thoroughly. As centuries of mud and dirt floated away in
the water of her bucket, Mrs Seaton suddenly went faint
with shock. What she was holding was not a powder
compact, but an ancient gold pendant, set with a sapphire
weighing almost ten carats!

Ted Seaton knew that the right thing to do was to

contact the authorities about his find, and soon the 'Middleham Jewel' was being examined by experts in medieval jewelry. They dated it to the fifteenth century, when Middleham Castle belonged to the powerful Earl of Warwick and later his son-in-law King Richard III. The jewel may have belonged to one of their friends or relatives. Its owner was probably a person who suffered ill-health, since it is inscribed with a charm to ward off attacks of epilepsy. It is easy to imagine a wealthy nobleman or woman riding out of the castle, perhaps on a hunting or hawking expedition, and not noticing that a weak link in the chain around their neck had given way. Later, they would have traced back over their path, hoping to see a gleam of gold by the wayside. But the jewel was gone, perhaps already trampled into the mud where it would remain for the next five hundred years.

An even more impressive find than the Middleham Jewel was made by Eric Lawes, in Suffolk, England, in 1992. While using his metal detector to look for a hammer which had been lost in a field, he instead came across a hoard of nearly fifteen thousand gold and silver coins! The money, together with some silver bowls, spoons and jewelry, had been carefully packed in a wooden chest and buried deep in the earth. Everything dated back to late Roman times, when

While using his metal detector to look for a hammer which had been lost in a field, he instead came across a hoard of nearly fifteen thousand gold and silver coins!

England was under threat from Saxon invaders. In the days before banks and safety deposit boxes, the owners of the treasure must have taken it out at night and buried it to keep it safe. But something went wrong. Perhaps they were killed or taken captive, or perhaps, having buried the treasure they were unable to find it again. One way or another, the treasure was never reclaimed, and today it can be seen in the British Museum.

Of course, whenever treasure is discovered, there is an argument as to who really owns it. In England, the law says that treasure which was deliberately hidden and never collected is called 'Treasure Trove' and becomes the property of the Crown. But treasure which is lost like the Middleham Jewel, and which cannot be traced to its original owner, becomes the joint property of the person who found it and the owner of the land on which it was found.

6

MYSTERIOUS CAVES

....

PAINTING THE DREAMTIME — ABORIGINAL ROCK ART

Today, Aboriginal art is very popular. It is sold in shops and art galleries both in Australia and overseas. Tourists travel thousands of miles to see famous examples of rock art in its original locations. Yet until quite recently, many people believed that Aboriginal art was ugly and worthless. Two people who have helped to change this opinion are Percy Trezise and Dick Roughsey, known to many Australians as the author and illustrator of popular books such as *The Giant Devil Dingo* and *The Magic Firesticks*.

Although today most people think of Percy Trezise as a writer, this was not always the way he earned his living. In fact, in the early 1960s, he was working as a pilot for Ansett in Far North Queensland. Unlike many white Australians of his generation, Percy Trezise had always been interested in Aboriginal culture. When he heard of a spectacular discovery of rock art near Laura, 120 miles northwest of Cairns, he was determined to find more about it. With his good friend, Aboriginal artist Dick Roughsey, Percy Trezise began exploring the country-side around Laura. Soon they realized that there was not one 'gallery' of rock art — there were dozens, some of them thousands of years old.

> **Soon they realized that there was not one 'gallery' of rock art — there were dozens, some of them thousands of years old.**

Over the next 25 years, the two friends devoted their lives to discovering, mapping and interpreting the Aboriginal rock paintings of Far North Queensland. Together, they found thousands of paintings of men and women, giant animals from the Dreamtime, and mysterious figures called Quinkins, regarded by the north Queensland Aboriginals as evil spirits. They traveled thousands of miles, camping out under the stars and living rough on 'bush tucker' (food from the wild), battling insects, deadly snakes and wild boars. Sometimes, Percy Trezise would take his family along with him. His two sons, Matthew and Stephen, even competed with each other to see who could find the best paintings! Elderly local Aboriginals accompanied them, explaining the meaning of the paintings wherever they could. Because Aboriginal tradition is passed on from generation to generation Percy

Trezise and Dick Roughsey knew that it was vital to write this information down before it was lost forever.

Many of the paintings discovered by the two friends referred to Dreamtime stories and traditions. Others had been used by Aboriginals for magic, for example, to ensure good hunting, or for a more sinister purpose. Sometimes, a person with a grudge against someone else would paint a picture of them dying a horrible death, and accompany the work with a powerful 'singing' to ensure the charm had the right effect. Paintings like this were usually done in secret, in case the victim or their family found out and tried to seek revenge. But in some cases, a crisis would prompt the entire tribe to action.

At two sites now called Pig Gallery and Emu Gallery, Percy Trezise and his companions discovered paintings of dead white men with rifles, their bodies being ripped apart by emus. Nobody knows what happened to the people who painted these pictures, but the magic was unsuccessful, and before long work on the beautiful paintings had stopped. During the gold rushes of the 1870s, thousands of European and Chinese miners flooded into Far North Queensland, hoping to make their fortunes. The Aboriginals tried to fight the invaders, but their spears were no match for guns, and many of them were killed. Later, in the 1920s, the Queensland government rounded up the remaining Aboriginal people. They broke up clans and families and sent them to reservations and mission stations far away from their traditional tribal homelands.

In 1985, Dick Roughsey died. Since then, Percy Trezise has continued their work alone, collecting information and publishing his discoveries in books and articles. By helping people learn about the fabulous Queensland paintings he hopes that all Australians, black and white, will find a new pride in one of the world's most important rock art collections.

ART GALLERY BENEATH THE SEA — THE COSQUER CAVE

It was a worrying time for the air-sea rescue team from Provence in southern France. Three divers had gone missing in the sea off Cape Morgiou, 7 miles southeast of Marseilles, and so far all attempts to find them had failed. Hope was fading quickly when Henri Cosquer, the owner of a local diving school, heard reports of what was happening and came forward with new information. He knew where the missing divers probably were, he told the rescuers — and the chances that they were still alive were bad.

With Henri Cosquer on board, the rescue boat motored out along the coast to the area where the divers had disappeared, and anchored alongside some limestone cliffs. Beneath the surface, Cosquer explained, was a cave — his own, private cave, which he had discovered six years before, and which he had been exploring ever since. The cave was one of the most dangerous he had ever seen, which was one of the reasons he had never told anyone about it. He suspected that the divers had accidentally found the entrance, and come to grief in the narrow passages beyond.

Cosquer and the rescue team put on their diving equipment and entered the tiny opening, little more than 3 feet high. Inside, pitch black if it had not been for their flashlights, was a long, narrow passage. Clouds of silt were stirred up by the divers' flippers as they passed, and the team quickly became disoriented. But Henri Cosquer knew where he was going. Soon, as he expected, they found the

> *Trapped and lost in the narrow tunnel, they had spent their last hours swimming frantically around in the darkness until finally they had run out of air and died.*

bodies of the three missing divers. Trapped and lost in the narrow tunnel, they had spent their last hours swimming frantically around in the darkness until finally they had run out of air and died.

Now that his cave had been discovered and a tragedy had occurred, Henri Cosquer knew that the authorities would seal its entrance off to prevent further accidents. But before they did, he knew that the cave's other secret — the reason he had been coming back to it for six whole years — would have to be shared with the rest of the world.

Signaling for the other divers to follow him, Henri Cosquer swam through a narrow crack in the rock at the end of the first passage. For 20 feet, the divers wriggled through another passage just over a metre high. At last, it opened out into a cave. The divers swam past submerged stalagmites up to 16 feet high until their heads broke surface in the middle of an underground lake. Here, if only they had been able to find it, was the air that could have saved the other divers' lives.

Henri Cosquer swam to the water's edge and climbed out into his secret cave, shining his flashlight over its walls. The other divers could only follow, then stare in amazement. Highlighted in the powerful beam of the diver's flashlight were paintings — wonderful paintings of animals, geometric shapes, and even human hands. They were looking at one of the most stunning collections of cave art found anywhere in the world. Henri Cosquer had discovered a Stone Age art gallery beneath the sea.

News of the spectacular find spread quickly. At first some experts were suspicious of how similar the cave's paintings looked to those in France's famous Lascaux Caves. They suspected the paintings were fakes — until dating tests proved their age beyond doubt. Henri Cosquer's story was also treated with suspicion because people could not understand how Stone Age people had entered an underwater cave. The answer to that question is actually quite simple. When the cave was in use, the sea level was much lower than it is today. Then the Ice Age came to an end and the great polar ice caps which had covered much of Europe slowly melted.

Over thousands of years the sea level rose until the mouth of the Cosquer Cave was under water, and its painted treasures were hidden from the outside world. In fact, although some paintings were probably lost when the water flooded in, cave art specialist Dr. Jean Clottes believes that the sea water in the entrance may actually have *helped* many of the paintings survive. By blocking out the outside air and light, it created a stable environment which prevented the paintings from decaying or fading.

Early people probably thought of the Cosquer Cave as a holy or magical place. They certainly never lived there, because although archaeologists have discovered charcoal from the fires they used to light their work, there are no signs of animal bones, tools, or any other Stone Age rubbish. About 28,000 years ago, cave artists started covering the walls with finger tracings, and stencils of their hands similar to those painted by Aboriginal people today. The oldest of these hands was dated to 25,000 B.C., and is the earliest hand-painting ever found.

Then, mysteriously, the cave was left deserted for thousands of years. We still don't know why. The cave's magic may have failed, or perhaps the people moved on to better hunting grounds and found somewhere else to paint their pictures. All we know for certain is that about 19,000 years ago people returned to the Cosquer Cave, and started using it again. This time they painted and carved the walls with hundreds of animals including horses, bison, deer and seals. Some of the animals were painted with spears sticking out of them. By painting pictures of wounded or dying animals, the people may have believed they would have success when they went hunting.

> *By painting pictures of wounded or dying animals, the people may have believed they would have success when they went hunting.*

Work on Henri Cosquer's wonderful art gallery under the sea continues today. However, because of the cave's dangerous entrance, progress has been slow. Only archaeologists who are trained divers can pass through the long, water-filled passage; a swim which takes twelve long minutes, fraught with danger all the way. Because of this, many of the world's greatest experts on cave art have not even seen the paintings. They can only view them on video screens, and use radio to direct the divers who are operating the cameras.

To prevent any more accidents, and to stop people from entering the cave and perhaps damaging the paintings, the mouth of the Cosquer Cave has been sealed. Some experts have suggested that a huge hole could be drilled through the roof of the cave to allow easier access. If this happens, archaeologists, and perhaps even the general public can enter and see the Cosquer paintings for themselves.

CITIES OF THE DEAD —
THE CATACOMBS OF ROME

Imagine, beneath the city where you live is another city — a city of the dead. Tunnels honeycomb the earth beneath your feet where thousands of bodies, wrapped in shrouds, lie rotting in niches in the walls. Around them, wall paintings and inscriptions wait in the darkness for your flashlight to pass over them, listing the names of thousands of people, once alive, now buried and forgotten in the blackness. Imagination? No. This city of the dead is a real place. You are in the catacombs — the burial places of ancient Rome.

In the early days of Roman civilization, dead people were usually cremated. Roman law did not allow burials inside the city, so when burials later became popular, cemeteries sprang up along the roadsides leading into the city. These cemeteries quickly became overcrowded, and were also haunted by robbers who attacked any travelers foolish enough to venture out at night. So, gradually, a new sort of graveyard came into existence — an *underground* graveyard or *catacomb*. These cities of the dead could hold thousands of bodies, and could also be carefully maintained and guarded.

Specialist grave-diggers called *fossores* began building a new catacomb by digging a tunnel into the earth (or sometimes into a hillside). They then constructed tall, narrow side-tunnels about 3 feet wide and 10 feet high. The walls of the tunnels were lined with niches for the bodies, stacked one on top of the other like enormous bunk beds. The Romans called these niches *loculi*, or recesses. Bigger tombs, which were designed to hold whole families, were called *cubicula*, which is related to the Latin word for 'bedroom'. In fact, the first catacombs were probably larger versions of the big family tombs which had always been built in Roman cemeteries.

As the niches filled up with bodies, more and more tunnels were dug, both off to the sides and on lower levels like a multi-level parking lot (some catacombs have as many as five or even seven levels). The fossores must often have got lost in the darkness and, sometimes, digging in an unfamiliar passage, they would break through unexpectedly into another tunnel, or even a neighboring catacomb. The digging was all done

by hand with picks and shovels, and must have been very hard work. The new fossore (who would probably have been quite a young boy) would also have found it rather frightening. The ancient Romans were very superstitious, and great believers in ghosts. The older men may have teased the newcomer, telling him frightful stories about spirits lurking in the dark, or suggesting that the sound of the workman's pick in the next tunnel was a dead man trying to get out of his grave. But the fossores would soon have got used to it, just as they would have learned to find their way through the hundreds of miles of dimly lit tunnels.

> *The ancient Romans were very superstitious, and great believers in ghosts. The older men may have teased the newcomer, telling him frightful stories about spirits lurking in the dark.*

Work would also have been difficult for the artists who painted the fine murals on the catacomb walls. The catacombs did have some natural light, for air-shafts were dug to prevent workers and visitors from suffocating underground, but most work would still have been done by lamp or torchlight. Many artists must have gone blind, or at least seriously damaged their eyesight by working in these conditions. Today, the paintings and inscriptions left by the mural artists help archaeologists to learn about the sort of people who were buried in the graves. For example, the grave of a Christian might be marked by a picture of

Jesus, or the secret Christian symbol of the fish.

Although people of all religions were buried in the catacombs, they have always been particularly associated with the early Christians. For many years people believed that Christians (who were being persecuted by the Roman government) would hide from the authorities in the catacombs, and even hold meetings there. This is a romantic story, and very unlikely in fact, as there would have been no room in the narrow passageways for large numbers of people to gather. Individual Christians *may* have hidden in the tunnels — but since they left no signs we have no real way of knowing whether they did or not. Later, when Christianity became more respectable, the catacombs were cared for by the Church. As a sign of respect, people would visit the graves of Christians who had been executed for refusing to give up their beliefs, and would perhaps have said a few prayers there. This habit may account for the later stories about meetings.

The great period of the Roman catacombs was between 200 and 400 A.D.. Towards the end of this time, people began burying their dead in open-air cemeteries again, and, gradually, the catacombs and those buried in them were forgotten. But today, visitors who go to Rome to see the marvelous ruins of the Roman Empire can also see the other cities beneath the ground — the cities of the dead where the Empire's citizens lie buried...

GLOSSARY

amphitheatre: an outside arena used for public contests or games, usually of oval or circular shape surrounded by tiered seats

aquanaut: a person working and temporarily living in an underwater research installation. Sometimes, the word is simply used to mean a skindiver

artifact: any object made by humans

borers: insects which burrow in wood, fruit etc., creating small holes and weakening the object

carrack: a large three-masted ship, usually fitted out for warfare

chronicler: a person who writes down events which occur, in order to leave a historical account for future generations

Druid: a priest among the ancient Celts of Britain, Ireland and France

excavation: a 'dig' undertaken by archaeologists and others who study the remains of ancient cultures

flagship: a ship which carries a flag officer, such as an admiral or rear admiral, and displays that person's flag

geologist: a person who studies the earth and the rocks it is made of

gladiator: a person, usually a slave or prisoner, who fought in ancient Rome in public as a form of entertainment

longbow: a bow over 6 feet long, used to fire feathered arrows

papyrus: a material for writing which is made from thin strips of the papyrus plant. Papyrus was used by the ancient Egyptians, Greeks and Romans

ziggurat: a temple in the shape of a pyramid which looks like a series of terraces

FURTHER READING

If you would like to find out more about some of the places mentioned in this book, the following list will help you. Most of the books are recently published, and should be available in public libraries; if not, ask your librarian to get them in for you. Some of the books were written for grownups. I have marked these with an asterisk, but you should still find them interesting.

General Books on Archaeology and Mysterious Places

The Master Builders
by Philip Wilkinson and
Michael Pollard
(Angus & Robertson, 1992)
(Includes Stonehenge, Troy, Machu Pichu and a number of other mysterious ruins.)

* *Vanished Civilizations*
(Readers Digest, 1983)
(includes Angkor, Pompeii and many other ancient cities.)

Cities: Troy and Pompeii

Secrets of Vesuvius
by C. Bisel
(___on, 1990)

Trojan War
by Elizabeth Edmondson
(Macmillan, 1992)

Pompeii: Nightmare at Midday
by Kathryn Long Humphrey
(Franklin Watts, 1990)

Underwater Treasure: the *Mary Rose* and the *Titanic*

So many books have been written about the *Titanic* disaster that you will be sure to find some in your local library. A few titles which might help you are:

Exploring the Titanic
by Robert Ballard
(Scholastic, 1988)

* *The Discovery of the* Titanic
by Robert Ballard
(Hodder & Stoughton, 1987)

The Sinking of the Titanic
by John Dudman
(Wayland, 1987)

* Titanic*: an Illustrated History*
by Don Lynch
(Hodder & Stoughton, 1992)
(This book has numerous photographs and excellent paintings reconstructing the disaster.)

* *The Search for Sunken Treasure: Exploring the World's Great Shipwrecks*
by Robert E. and Jennifer Marx
(Random House, 1993)
(This is a general book on shipwrecks and underwater archaeology. It mentions both the *Titanic* and the *Mary Rose*.)

The Mary Rose*: her Wreck and Rescue*
by Ian Morrison
(Lutterworth, 1983)

Mysterious Stone Monuments

Easter Island: The Island of Stone Giants
Sheila McCullagh
(Longman, 1979)

Pyramids of East and West

New titles about the Egyptian Pyramids are being written all the time. A few suggestions for further reading include:

Pyramids of Ancient Egypt
by John D. Clare
(Random House, 1991)

Pyramids
by Anne Millard
(Franklin Watts, 1989)

Inside an Egyptian Pyramid
by Jacqueline Morley et al.
(Simon & Schuster, 1991)

The Mayas
by Robert Nicholson
(Macmillan, 1993)

The Mayas
by Pamela Odijk
(Macmillan, 1989)

The Sumerians
by Pamela Odijk
(Macmillan, 1989)

Egyptian Pyramids
by Anne Steel
(Wayland, 1989)

Treasure and Treasure-Seeker

There are no books as yet about the rediscovery of the Trojan Gold. If you would like to find out about how to use a metal detector, the following book will be useful:

* *Metal Detecting for Gold and Relic in Australia*
Douglas M. Stone and Bob Sar
(Outdoor Press, 1987)

Mysterious Caves

There are no books yet about Cosquer Cave, but the follow on Aboriginal rock paintings reading:

* *Dream Road*
by Percy Trezise
(Allen & Unwin, 1993)

INDEX

m 856 - J
808